# Which _____ Are You?

## Quiz Book

by Aubre Andrus
illustrated by Jennifer Kalis

Published by American Girl Publishing

16 17 18 19 20 21 LEO 11 10 9 8 7

Editorial Development: Mary Richards Beaumont
Art Direction & Design: Sarah Boecher, Gretchen Becker
Production: Tami Kepler, Judith Lary, Paula Moon, Kristi Tabrizi
Illustrations: Jennifer Kalis

americangirl.com/service

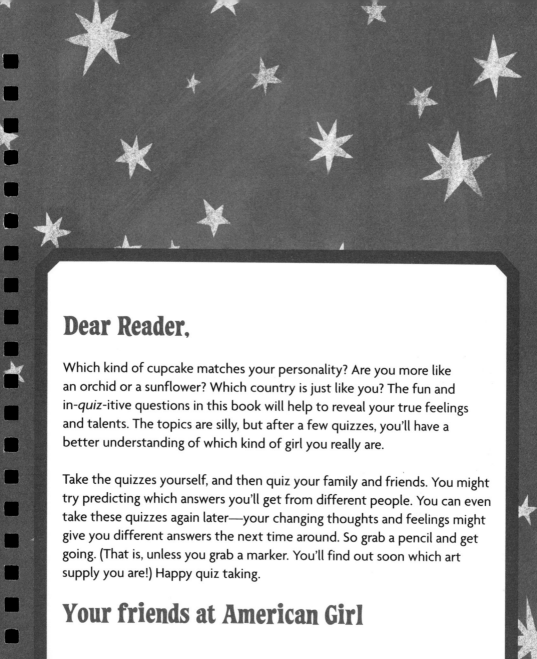

# Dear Reader,

Which kind of cupcake matches your personality? Are you more like an orchid or a sunflower? Which country is just like you? The fun and in-*quiz*-itive questions in this book will help to reveal your true feelings and talents. The topics are silly, but after a few quizzes, you'll have a better understanding of which kind of girl you really are.

Take the quizzes yourself, and then quiz your family and friends. You might try predicting which answers you'll get from different people. You can even take these quizzes again later—your changing thoughts and feelings might give you different answers the next time around. So grab a pencil and get going. (That is, unless you grab a marker. You'll find out soon which art supply you are!) Happy quiz taking.

# Your friends at American Girl

# Table of Contents

# Which City Are You?

Cities have personalities just as we do! Uncover which city is most like you.

**1.** When I dream about my future home, I see myself in a . . .
- **a.** big city with bright lights.
- **b.** laid-back beach town.
- **c.** picturesque place.
- **d.** friendly neighborhood.

**2.** My ideal closet would be filled with . . .
- **a.** cool purses and trendy boots.
- **b.** flip-flops and sundresses.
- **c.** hiking boots and bandannas.
- **d.** comfy T-shirts and sneakers.

**3.** You'd never find me . . .
- **a.** skiing down a mountain.
- **b.** wearing a gown at a fancy ball.
- **c.** inside on a sunny day.
- **d.** without my friends and family nearby.

**4.** In my hometown, I wish we had more . . .
- **a.** places to shop.
- **b.** sunny and warm weather.
- **c.** public parks and trails.
- **d.** history and sights to see.

**5.** In my family, we love to share . . .
- **a.** fashion advice.
- **b.** an afternoon together outside.
- **c.** tips on how to play our favorite sports better.
- **d.** recipes—then we cook them together.

**6.** I would love to move to a place with . . .
- **a.** some of the tallest buildings in the world.
- **b.** lots of sunshine.
- **c.** lots of snow.
- **d.** people who are known for being friendly.

**7.** For a special meal out, I'd love to go to . . .
- **a.** a sushi restaurant where I can try something new.
- **b.** a diner where the servers sing and dance.
- **c.** an outdoor patio where I can eat under the stars.
- **d.** a family-owned place with yummy comfort food such as mac and cheese.

**8.** I get inspired when I . . .
- **a.** am really busy and have tons of things to do.
- **b.** see a beautiful sunset.
- **c.** get active outside.
- **d.** meet interesting people.

**9.** One day, I'd love to have a job . . .
- **a.** at a big, world-famous company.
- **b.** with an office overlooking the ocean.
- **c.** that lets me bring my dog to work.
- **d.** where I know everyone and they know me.

**10.** Sometimes people tell me that I . . .
- **a.** talk too fast. It's always go, go, go with me!
- **b.** am easygoing and up for anything.
- **c.** can solve any problem. I'm good at figuring things out!
- **d.** can get along with anyone. I'm naturally friendly!

## Answers start on page 54.

# Which Cupcake Are You?

Sprinkles and frosting and sugar—oh, my! What does your party style say about you?

**1.** When I choose a birthday cake, I pick . . .
   **a.** the wildest flavor combination I can find.
   **b.** a plain cake that I can decorate myself.
   **c.** a themed cake with my favorite character or animal.
   **d.** half chocolate, half vanilla to please everyone.

**2.** At a friend's birthday party, I'm the girl who . . .
   **a.** is talking the loudest.
   **b.** makes a handmade present for the birthday girl.
   **c.** is playing with the birthday girl's pet hamster.
   **d.** makes sure everyone is included in the party games.

**3.** If I lose at a party game, I'll . . .
   **a.** suggest a different game that I'd rather play.
   **b.** say nothing but give a smile to show that I'm OK.
   **c.** congratulate the winner on a job well done.
   **d.** cheer on my friends no matter what.

**4.** If I see a karaoke machine at a party, I'll . . .
   **a.** grab the microphone and sing my heart out.
   **b.** avoid singing unless someone will do it with me.
   **c.** join a friend if she seems too scared to sing by herself.
   **d.** gather everyone to sing a song as a group.

**5.** You can tell which present I gave the birthday girl by the . . .

   **a.** huge burst of curly ribbons on top—it's eye-catching!

   **b.** thought I put into the gift—it's unique.

   **c.** stuffed animal inside—I love to give cuddly "friends."

   **d.** reaction of the birthday girl—it's just what she wanted.

**6.** At a sleepover, I'm usually the one who . . .

   **a.** brings the best games and movies.

   **b.** invents new games for everyone to play.

   **c.** gets a little homesick for my family and dog.

   **d.** hosts the party and invites everyone over.

**7.** When I plan my birthday party, I . . .

   **a.** want the theme to be simple: "Let's have fun!"

   **b.** make my own unique theme and decorations.

   **c.** choose a theme around animals such as dogs, horses, or monkeys.

   **d.** pick out a popular theme at the party store.

**8.** If there's a missing goody bag and my friend doesn't get one, I . . .

   **a.** tell a joke to help make her feel better.

   **b.** ask everyone to donate one goody-bag item to her.

   **c.** give her half of the treats in my goody bag.

   **d.** give her my bag to cheer her up.

Thanks for Coming!

**9.** If I don't get invited to a friend's birthday party, I . . .

   **a.** don't mind because I have other friends.

   **b.** am disappointed but don't say anything about it.

   **c.** understand that she could invite only a few friends.

   **d.** will still invite her to my birthday party.

# Which Movie Style Are You?

The star of this quiz is YOU!

**1.** When it comes to movies, I don't like it when . . .
  **a.** there's not enough action.
  **b.** it's too suspenseful.
  **c.** nothing gives me goosebumps.
  **d.** the ending is too easy to figure out.

**2.** If I were to direct my own movie, it would definitely have a . . .
  **a.** lot of special effects.
  **b.** happy ending.
  **c.** major surprise.
  **d.** tricky or clever plot.

**3.** I love movies that . . .
  **a.** show me new places around the world.
  **b.** put me in a good mood.
  **c.** make me jump out of my seat.
  **d.** have a mystery to solve.

**4.** The best part about being a movie star would be . . .
  **a.** doing my own stunts.
  **b.** wearing gowns on a red carpet.
  **c.** getting to wear different costumes and makeup.
  **d.** acting out interesting stories.

**5.** My dream job is to be . . .
  **a.** a superstar athlete.
  **b.** a writer of young-adult novels.
  **c.** a theme-park designer.
  **d.** a detective who solves big cases.

**6.** My favorite place to see a movie is . . .
  **a.** a theater with a great sound system.
  **b.** a drive-in movie theater under the stars.
  **c.** a multiplex with a big group of friends.
  **d.** my family room, where I can watch without distractions.

**7.** If I starred in a movie, I would love to play the . . .
  **a.** heroine who saves the day.
  **b.** silly best friend.
  **c.** villain.
  **d.** brainy sleuth who helps solve a problem.

**8.** If an audience were watching a movie I directed, I would want them to . . .
  **a.** cheer at the end.
  **b.** cry during my heartwarming story.
  **c.** scream at least once.
  **d.** ponder how the movie will end.

**9.** When a new movie comes out, I . . .
  **a.** gather up my friends to see it in 3-D.
  **b.** want to read the book first.
  **c.** am the first in line on opening night.
  **d.** don't like when the trailer gives too much information.

**10.** Sometimes I wish I could . . .
  **a.** visit the exciting world created in my favorite movie.
  **b.** be friends with the characters on-screen.
  **c.** dive into the movie to help the characters in danger.
  **d.** get an award for writing an awesome screenplay.

# Which Art Supply Are You?

Do you take chances or play it safe? How you react to these creative conundrums will tell you what kind of art supply you are.

**1.** It's time to make a sculpture in art class. You . . .
- **a.** pretty much copy the teacher's example.
- **b.** get to work immediately and don't care if you mess up.
- **c.** glance around the room timidly, but then try your best.
- **d.** make the tallest sculpture in the class.

**2.** If you were allowed to decorate your room however you'd like, you would . . .
- **a.** consult your friends for advice first.
- **b.** change the whole thing from top to bottom with no plan.
- **c.** add a karaoke machine like your best friend's.
- **d.** pull out a sketch of a dream room you've been designing for years.

**3.** At a birthday party, a friend lays out an assortment of art supplies and says you can make anything. You . . .
- **a.** feel completely overwhelmed and end up drawing a birthday cake.
- **b.** find matching beads and create pretty bracelets for yourself and your mom.
- **c.** ask a friend to help you make a simple paper chain for decoration.
- **d.** create a huge, sparkly party crown for the birthday girl.

**4.** Your book report is due next week, and you don't know where to begin. You decide to . . .
  a. see what your friends are doing for their projects.
  b. create a diorama, even though you've never made one before.
  c. keep it simple and make a pretty poster for your presentation.
  d. perform a scene from the book, complete with costumes and props.

**5.** When it comes to doing crafts, you'd prefer having . . .
  a. a class with a teacher to help you along the way.
  b. a random assortment of pretty fabrics and cool buttons.
  c. a book with step-by-step instructions.
  d. a great big pile of mismatched art supplies.

**6.** In gym class, your teacher asks the students to choreograph group dances. You . . .
  a. hope your friends have some ideas, because you don't even know how to start.
  b. take the lead—it's a fun challenge!
  c. teach your friends a few moves from a dance class you took.
  d. start freestyle dancing and ask your friends to pick their favorite moves.

**7.** Your parents ask you to write something nice in your grandpa's birthday card. You . . .
  a. sign your name but don't know what else to write.
  b. come up with a short rhyming poem about his birthday.
  c. write "Hope it's a great one!" and sign your name.
  d. don't sign it because you already sent him a handmade card.

# Which Video Game Are You?

Your new quest is to find your playing personality.

**1.** When it comes to puzzles, I . . .
- Ⓐ would rather play a board game with a friend.
- Ⓑ try to solve them but then get distracted by something else.
- Ⓒ need to set a timer to challenge myself or I'll get bored.
- Ⓓ can't stop until I'm finished— even if it takes all afternoon.

**2.** In a competition, I'm a great teammate because I . . .
- Ⓐ am not afraid to take a chance.
- Ⓑ work hard but have fun while I'm doing it.
- Ⓒ am very competitive and like to win.
- Ⓓ can figure out a winning strategy.

**3.** If I missed a game-winning shot for my team, I would most likely . . .
- Ⓐ remind my teammates that we still played well.
- Ⓑ practice so that I'd be more prepared for the next game.
- Ⓒ be inspired to try even harder next time.
- Ⓓ know that I tried my best, which is all that I could do.

**4.** If I were given an activity book, I would flip right to the . . .
- Ⓐ jokes and riddles.
- Ⓑ "find the differences" picture puzzles.
- Ⓒ biggest maze in the book.
- Ⓓ crossword puzzles.

**5.** My favorite reality shows are . . .
- Ⓐ talent competitions with amazing performers.
- Ⓑ funny video shows that make me laugh.
- Ⓒ ones that have players race to complete a task.
- Ⓓ game shows where players win prizes for correct answers.

**6.** When playing a game, I get really excited when I . . .
- Ⓐ get a chance to show off a little.
- Ⓑ don't have to follow all the rules.
- Ⓒ see the competition closing in on me.
- Ⓓ know exactly what to do next.

**7.** It might be scary to some people, but I'm not afraid to . . .
- Ⓐ perform in public.
- Ⓑ make myself look silly.
- Ⓒ challenge a competitor.
- Ⓓ think quickly under pressure.

**8.** When I'm doing homework, you might find me . . .
- Ⓐ humming quietly to myself.
- Ⓑ tapping my foot impatiently.
- Ⓒ racing through the questions so I can finish quickly.
- Ⓓ double-checking all of my answers.

**9.** My friends tell me I'm great at . . .
- Ⓐ being brave and trying new things.
- Ⓑ making other people laugh.
- Ⓒ making things (such as crafts) with my hands.
- Ⓓ remembering the answers to tricky trivia questions.

**10.** I'm proud of the fact that I am good at . . .
- Ⓐ following directions.
- Ⓑ picking up on things quickly.
- Ⓒ working under pressure, such as when I'm finishing a test before the bell rings.
- Ⓓ solving problems.

# Which Drink Are You?

Take this quiz to find out which super sipper excites your taste buds.

1. When it comes to breakfast, some people think I'm weird for eating . . .
   a. pizza.
   b. chocolate-chip pancakes.
   c. the same cereal every morning.
   d. a veggie-filled omelet.

2. My favorite place to buy food is at the . . .
   a. deli—I could eat a sandwich or salad for every meal.
   b. bakery—there are so many treats to choose from.
   c. grocery store—I know exactly what brands I like.
   d. farmers' market—all the fruits and veggies look so fresh.

3. For a birthday treat to share with my class, I like to bring in . . .
   a. big soft pretzels.
   b. cupcakes with sprinkles on top.
   c. my grandma's chocolate-chip cookies.
   d. strawberries dipped in chocolate.

4. I would rather eat . . .
   a. potato chips instead of chocolate.
   b. dessert instead of dinner.
   c. plain cheese pizza—no onions and no spices.
   d. a granola bar instead of a candy bar.

**5.** When my family goes out to dinner, I tend to . . .

   **a.** ask if we can order an appetizer.

   **b.** beg to go out for ice cream afterward.

   **c.** order my favorite dish every time.

   **d.** clean my entire plate!

**6.** When someone offers me food that I haven't tried before, I . . .

   **a.** try one bite—especially if it's savory or salty.

   **b.** try one bite, but only if it's going to taste sweet.

   **c.** fib and tell people that I'm allergic to it.

   **d.** always take a few bites—I'll try anything.

**7.** In my dream room, there would be a . . .

   **a.** phone with a direct line to a french-fry delivery service.

   **b.** jewelry box filled with candy rings and necklaces.

   **c.** PB&J sandwich dispenser next to my bed.

   **d.** sunny windowsill for growing herbs.

**8.** If I opened my own food cart, I would serve . . .

   **a.** tiny burgers with all the toppings.

   **b.** fancy sodas in every flavor imaginable.

   **c.** mini grilled-cheese sandwiches with cups of tomato soup.

   **d.** healthy snacks such as hummus and carrots.

**9.** They say, "You are what you eat," so I guess I'm . . .

   **a.** nutty.

   **b.** sweet.

   **c.** simple.

   **d.** fresh.

**10.** When it comes to comfort food, nothing comes close to . . .

   **a.** a big bowl of macaroni.

   **b.** apple pie, warm from the oven.

   **c.** a simple turkey sandwich.

   **d.** freshly picked raspberries.

# Which Plant Are You?

You've already blossomed into a beautiful person. Take this quiz to find out which plant grows your way.

**1.** A friend tells you she doesn't like your brand-new shirt. You . . .
- **a.** stand up for yourself and tell her why you like it.
- **b.** don't care. It's just her opinion.
- **c.** put on a smile and change the subject.
- **d.** ignore her comment and start talking to your other friends.

**2.** Sometimes you dream about being . . .
- **a.** a gymnast who has strength and grace.
- **b.** a swimmer who has speed and ease.
- **c.** a runner who has energy and determination.
- **d.** a teacher who has smarts and dedication.

**3.** This summer, you're going to a week-long horse camp. You can't wait to . . .
- **a.** meet new people.
- **b.** spend time relaxing outside.
- **c.** go riding in the warm weather.
- **d.** learn something new.

**4.** When it comes to after-school activities, you . . .
- **a.** campaign to be president of the science club.
- **b.** prefer to spend time at home studying and reading.
- **c.** join any sport that lets you run in the sun.
- **d.** can't pick just one!

**5.** Your friends put in a DVD that you're too scared to watch. You . . .
  a. tell them that you're too scared to watch it.
  b. suggest another movie that you know everyone likes.
  c. ask if they want to play a game instead of watching the movie.
  d. decide to give it a try—maybe you'll like it.

**6.** When it comes to your style, you like to wear clothes that . . .
  a. really give you a unique look.
  b. are nice and simple.
  c. are comfortable and let you move.
  d. can switch easily from school to lacrosse practice.

**7.** If you were shipwrecked on a deserted island, the first thing you'd do would be to . . .
  a. build a hut.
  b. go for a walk in the forest.
  c. stretch out on the beach.
  d. make a list of things to do.

**8.** You get a bad grade on a test. You . . .
  a. tell your parents that you'll study harder next time.
  b. ask a friend to explain the correct answers to you.
  c. decide to form a study group for the next test.
  d. reschedule your activities so that you'll have more time to study.

# Which Animal Are You?

Answer these questions to reveal which critter you can relate to.

**1.** In a "fun emergency kit," I'd pack . . .
- **a.** my family's favorite board games.
- **b.** sports equipment to help me stay active.
- **c.** a stack of books to read.
- **d.** a cell phone with all of my friends' phone numbers.

**2.** I feel as if I have a sixth sense because I can . . .
- **a.** tell when something is wrong with a family member.
- **b.** play even harder when I know that I'm about to lose.
- **c.** tune out loud noises and focus completely on what I'm doing.
- **d.** usually find ways to make my friends laugh.

**3.** On a summer weekend, you'll find me . . .
- **a.** spending quality time with my siblings.
- **b.** at basketball camp learning how to shoot better.
- **c.** lying in the yard and looking at things from a bug's point of view.
- **d.** at the neighborhood pool all day.

**4.** When my family went on a cruise, I spent as much time as I could . . .
- **a.** taking family pictures—we made some great memories.
- **b.** trying new things—I learned how to play shuffleboard.
- **c.** enjoying the views—they were amazing.
- **d.** meeting new friends—I'm not afraid to say hi.

**5.** My all-time favorite game is . . .
 a. kickball—I love diving for the ball.
 b. a relay race, because it's so exciting.
 c. solitaire, because I can play it on my own wherever I want.
 d. any board game played with a big group.

**6.** I think life's always more fun when . . .
 a. there's time to play!
 b. there's a goal I'm trying to reach.
 c. I feel confident in myself.
 d. I have friends by my side.

**7.** If I had to pick a "uniform" for myself, it would be . . .
 a. jeans, a T-shirt, and sneakers.
 b. warm-up pants and a matching jacket.
 c. a cozy sweater and slippers.
 d. flip-flops, sunglasses, and a swimsuit cover-up.

**8.** When I visit a museum, I love to . . .
 a. take my time interacting with each exhibit.
 b. try to see as many exhibits as quickly as I can.
 c. roam freely on my own and visit only the exhibits that interest me.
 d. go with a few friends so that we can talk about the fascinating things we learn.

**9.** Over the weekend, my family and I love to go to . . .
 a. a park, where we can goof off and play games.
 b. a baseball game, where we can cheer on our home team.
 c. a movie theater, where we can watch a great story.
 d. an aquarium, where we can gape at the amazing displays.

# Which Experiment Are You?

We have a hypothesis—how you answer these questions says a lot about YOU. Take this quiz to discover the results.

**1.** If you were to make your own birthday cake, you would . . .
- **a.** personalize a recipe by adding a few interesting ingredients.
- **b.** patiently follow your mom's special recipe step-by-step.
- **c.** research a cool new recipe that your friends will love.
- **d.** decorate a pre-made cake with rainbow frosting and an assortment of candy.

**2.** Your favorite kind of book is . . .
- **a.** choose-your-path stories with multiple endings.
- **b.** fantasy stories—especially the really long ones.
- **c.** books about history and what life was like for real people.
- **d.** graphic novels with lots of action and suspense.

**3.** You're definitely not afraid of . . .
   **a.** taking a chance on something new.
   **b.** taking extra care to do something right the first time.
   **c.** discovering something on your own.
   **d.** getting your hands a little dirty.

**4.** Someday, you'd like to conduct research on . . .
   **a.** what happens when you ride a roller coaster backward.
   **b.** how long it takes the lake to freeze before you can ice skate on it.
   **c.** whether some junk foods are actually good for you.
   **d.** how fast you could eat an ice-cream sundae with no hands.

**5.** At a make-your-own-pizza party, you'd . . .
   **a.** pick a topping, such as pineapple, that you've never tried before.
   **b.** carefully place a perfect pattern of sausage and pepperoni.
   **c.** take a poll to find out what everyone's favorite toppings are.
   **d.** cover your eyes and pick the first five ingredients you touch.

**6.** When painting a self-portrait in art class, you . . .
   **a.** create a painting that's half you, half your pet dog.
   **b.** focus and really concentrate while you work.
   **c.** help a friend to paint her eyes and mouth just right.
   **d.** are covered with paint by the end of class. Oh well!

**7.** You would love an activity kit that showed you how to . . .
   **a.** build an alarm clock that wakes you up with nice smells.
   **b.** take care of an indoor herb garden.
   **c.** turn sunlight into a rainbow.
   **d.** make a tie-dye T-shirt.

**8.** You wish you knew how to . . .
   **a.** make your own freeze-dried "astronaut" ice cream.
   **b.** gather solar energy for your house.
   **c.** predict the weather based on cloud formations.
   **d.** build a remote-controlled airplane.

**9.** When playing a board game, you like to . . .
   **a.** make up your own rules to give the game a new twist.
   **b.** read all the directions aloud so that everyone understands.
   **c.** introduce your friends to a game they've never played before.
   **d.** break into teams—it's more fun.

# Which Accessory Are You?

Style is a personal choice. Find out which extra expresses YOU.

**1.** Your friends don't know it, but you are . . .
  **a.** afraid to get your ears pierced.
  **b.** bringing friendship bracelets for all of them to school tomorrow.
  **c.** not a big fan of pink—which is their favorite color.
  **d.** wearing a skirt tomorrow that you made yourself.

**2.** It sounds kind of crazy, but one day you'd love to . . .
  **a.** star in a play, even though you're pretty shy.
  **b.** write your own song and play it at school.
  **c.** join the basketball team, even though none of your friends play.
  **d.** dye your hair pink.

**3.** Your grandma bought you an *interesting* sweater for your birthday. You . . .
 a. hide it—you don't want anyone to see this.
 b. wear it to a family party—after all, it's the thought that counts.
 c. will think about wearing it—but probably won't.
 d. layer it with a jacket—it actually looks kind of cute.

**4.** When you show up at school carrying a messenger bag you decorated yourself, your friends . . .
 a. make you blush when they compliment you.
 b. are not surprised—you're always making cool things!
 c. are surprised since you usually keep things plain.
 d. immediately want to know how to make one themselves.

**5.** Last year, you had a roller-skating birthday party. This year . . .
 a. you're going to have a small sleepover at home.
 b. you want to try something new, such as laser tag.
 c. you're going to do it again because it was fun.
 d. a few of your friends want to try the same idea.

**6.** You just got a haircut, and your friends . . .
 a. don't notice because you put your hair in a ponytail.
 b. immediately notice your new cut—it's very different!
 c. don't notice because you got just a trim.
 d. love your new short hair and ask where you got it done.

**7.** Your friends can always count on you to . . .
 a. keep a secret—you won't tell a soul.
 b. be up for anything—you're a free spirit.
 c. just hang out—you don't need to do anything special to have fun.
 d. stand up for them—you're a caring person.

**8.** For your school's holiday play, you have to dress up as a tree. You . . .
 a. are horrified that you have to wear the silly costume.
 b. think it's hilarious and can't wait to perform.
 c. feel better that five others will be wearing the same costume.
 d. put a smile on your face and make the best of it.

# Which Word Are You?

You already know that you're *funny, smart,* and *nice.* Find out which one of these more interesting words describes you.

**1.** When it comes to my friends, I can . . .
- a. almost make them squirt milk out of their noses because they're laughing so hard.
- b. astound them with an interesting fact.
- c. give a little pep talk when they're feeling down.
- d. make time for anyone—friends and family come first.

**2.** I can't imagine going one day without . . .
- a. making someone smile.
- b. having a great conversation with a friend.
- c. trying to be better at something than I was the day before.
- d. doing a good deed.

**3.** My friends like to tease me for . . .
- a. being too giggly—I like to laugh!
- b. talking too much—I can't help it!
- c. being too competitive—I like to win!
- d. rescuing everything—I love all animals!

**4.** In school, I enjoy group projects because I . . .
- a. am fun to work with.
- b. am comfortable speaking in front of the class.
- c. am a good leader.
- d. get along with everybody.

**5.** Sometimes I find it hard to . . .
- a. take things seriously.
- b. keep quiet when I need to.
- c. be OK with losing.
- d. compete against my friends.

**6.** You'll never find my friends and me . . .

   a. without a smile—we're always having a great time.

   b. quietly watching a movie—we're a little loud.

   c. sitting still for an afternoon—we like to keep moving.

   d. leaving anyone out—we include everyone.

**7.** My family says that one day I'll be . . .

   a. a performer, because I like to entertain others.

   b. a TV reporter, because I love to tell stories.

   c. a professional athlete, because I love to train hard.

   d. a doctor, because I love to care for others.

**8.** I'm the only one of my friends who'd be able to . . .

   a. successfully babysit for a few bored kids.

   b. give a speech to a huge audience.

   c. stay on a balance beam.

   d. easily make new friends in a room full of strangers.

**9.** In my free time, I like to . . .

   a. play outside with my younger siblings.

   b. spend quality time catching up with my mom or dad.

   c. solve puzzles or games that make me think hard.

   d. make crafts that I end up giving to my best friends.

**10.** I would rather . . .

   a. run a mile than take a test.

   b. star onstage than be in the audience.

   c. compete by myself than with a team.

   d. give gifts than receive them.

# Which Volunteer Are You?

Learn how you can put your interests, skills, and dreams to work as a volunteer.

1. I think it's important that we all try to . . .
   a. save endangered animals.
   b. inspire others to dream big.
   c. help less fortunate people in times of need.
   d. make the world a "greener" place.

2. I get inspired when I hear a story about . . .
   a. a friend who visits her grandma in a nursing home every week.
   b. someone who worked really hard for her success.
   c. families who adopt another family over the holidays and donate gifts.
   d. a school that's planting trees for Earth Day.

3. If I were to win $1 million, I would use some of the money to build . . .
   a. an animal hospital in my hometown.
   b. a school in Africa.
   c. a grocery store in a neighborhood that didn't have one.
   d. a public park in a city.

4. Sometimes I like to remind myself . . .
   a. to put others before myself.
   b. that nothing is impossible.
   c. that I'm lucky to have everything I do.
   d. to leave the world a better place than I found it.

**5.** I like to dream that one day, I'll . . .
   **a.** foster dogs and cats until they find their "forever" homes.
   **b.** coach a sports team and help them win a championship.
   **c.** organize an art auction to raise money for a kids' charity.
   **d.** invent a process that turns plastic bags into fabric for clothes.

**6.** I once had a birthday party . . .
   **a.** for my pet dog!
   **b.** at which we wore costumes that showed what we wanted to be when we grow up.
   **c.** and asked for donations to a charity instead of presents.
   **d.** during which we recycled "trash" into clever crafts.

**7.** I feel as if I'm helping most when I'm . . .
   **a.** spending time with someone face-to-face.
   **b.** attending a charity event.
   **c.** donating my time or resources to a great cause.
   **d.** able to see the difference I've made.

**8.** My friends tell me that I'm very . . .
   **a.** friendly and easy to get along with.
   **b.** confident and positive.
   **c.** gracious and appreciative for everything.
   **d.** responsible and aware of how my actions affect others.

**9.** I'm the kind of girl who . . .
   **a.** always wears a smile.
   **b.** tells my friend, "Great job!" when she gets an A on a test.
   **c.** will give my bracelet to a friend if she really likes it.
   **d.** picks up garbage when I see it on the sidewalk.

FOOD Bank DONATIONS

# Which Vacation Are You?

Unpack your travel tendencies—they'll show whether you're a beach bum or an amazing adventurer.

**1.** You have just arrived in a new city by yourself. You . . .
  **a.** are nervous and call your parents.
  **b.** grab a map and research what to do first.
  **c.** find the nearest café where you can people-watch.
  **d.** rent a bike and start exploring.

**2.** If you don't recognize anything on a menu, you . . .
  **a.** ask if the chef can make your favorite dish.
  **b.** take a chance on something new.
  **c.** ask the server to bring you the restaurant's best dish.
  **d.** order a sample platter so that you can try a bit of everything.

**3.** On a long road trip, you wouldn't survive without a . . .
  **a.** backpack filled with books, games, and an MP3 player.
  **b.** friend to experience it with you.
  **c.** comfy pillow and blanket.
  **d.** good view out the window.

**4.** You've just landed in Paris! You . . .
  **a.** sign up for a guided bicycle tour.
  **b.** order a crêpe—in French. (You've been practicing!)
  **c.** take a stroll along the River Seine.
  **d.** race to the Eiffel Tower.

**5.** When it comes to vacations, you like it when your family . . .
  **a.** visits your cousins who live across the country.
  **b.** goes to a theme park with the tallest roller coasters.
  **c.** relaxes at your grandparents' cabin on a lake.
  **d.** hikes through national parks.

**6.** You could see yourself one day . . .
  **a.** being a great "armchair traveler" who reads about faraway places.
  **b.** moving abroad and learning to speak a new language.
  **c.** opening your own bed-and-breakfast on an island.
  **d.** as a survival-skills expert who can live easily in the wilderness.

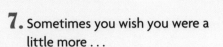

**7.** Sometimes you wish you were a little more . . .
  a. brave.
  b. organized.
  c. adventurous.
  d. patient.

**8.** It doesn't feel like a vacation unless you . . .
  a. spend time with your family.
  b. have to bring a passport.
  c. are wearing a bathing suit.
  d. spend all day outside.

**9.** When a rainy day changes your travel plans, you . . .
  a. get upset and don't know what to do next.
  b. decide that you'll head to some museums.
  c. spend the afternoon curled up on the couch, relaxing.
  d. get cabin fever—you don't like being cooped up all day.

**10.** The best travel souvenirs are . . .
  a. ticket stubs from all the fun things you did with your family.
  b. pictures that show all the amazing places you've visited.
  c. seashells that you gathered— now you can listen to the ocean anytime!
  d. a worn-out pair of hiking boots.

# Which Character Are You?

Find out which fantasy character is most like the REAL you.

**1.** In my group of friends, I'm the one who always . . .
   **a.** knows the perfect thing to say—almost like magic.
   **b.** stands up to any bully.
   **c.** gives support by cheering them on at games.
   **d.** offers wise advice to those in need.

**2.** It's true that I'm the girl most likely to have . . .
   **a.** started a recycling program at my school.
   **b.** saved my dog from running into a busy street.
   **c.** helped a friend practice for a spelling bee.
   **d.** entered a story contest.

**3.** My favorite stories are . . .
   **a.** with magic spells and enchanted objects.
   **b.** in which good defeats evil.
   **c.** in which dreams come true.
   **d.** about faraway lands that come to life in my imagination.

**4.** Sometimes I have problems . . .
- **a.** making a decision—I have so many ideas.
- **b.** being patient when teaching others something new.
- **c.** balancing friends, homework, family, sports, and school.
- **d.** paying attention in class—I drift into daydreams.

**5.** When a friend needs help, I . . .
- **a.** can come up with a way to make her feel better.
- **b.** am immediately at her side, no matter what.
- **c.** constantly check up on her to make sure she's OK.
- **d.** tell her what she needs to hear—even if it's hard to say.

**6.** Compared to my other friends, I'm a lot more . . .
- **a.** resourceful—nothing stumps me.
- **b.** outspoken—I'm not afraid to say what I think.
- **c.** caring—I'm aware of how my actions affect others.
- **d.** mature—sometimes I feel older than I am.

**7.** If someone could jump into my mind, she'd see that I'm always . . .
- **a.** thinking—it's hard to turn off my brain and relax.
- **b.** very aware of what's going on around me.
- **c.** worrying about others too much.
- **d.** imagining what my next project should be.

**8.** One day, when I'm older, I'd love to . . .
- **a.** invent unmeltable ice cream.
- **b.** be a role model for younger kids.
- **c.** donate lots of money to charity.
- **d.** have one of my paintings in an art museum.

**9.** Sometimes I wish that I could . . .
- **a.** get what I want with the wave of a wand.
- **b.** fly around the world with ease.
- **c.** listen in on conversations like a fly on a wall.
- **d.** be amazingly skillful at lots of different things.

# Which Ball Are You?

Feeling a little competitive? See how your personality plays out in this match.

**1.** When it comes to video games, I prefer to play . . .
- **a.** to win! Or at least to set a new high score.
- **b.** something new—with a little practice, I'll get the hang of it.
- **c.** with a partner—it's more fun to play together.
- **d.** a silly dancing or singing game with friends.

**2.** If I were to get a bronze medal in a competition, I would be . . .
- **a.** sad that I didn't get a gold medal.
- **b.** happy as long as I tried my best.
- **c.** nice to the winners and congratulate them.
- **d.** proud that I got a medal.

**3.** Before a big game, I'm the girl most likely to be . . .
- **a.** spending the last few minutes practicing on the sidelines.
- **b.** volunteering to change positions at the last minute.
- **c.** leading the team cheer before we run onto the court.
- **d.** asking my teammates what they're doing after the game.

**4.** If I had to run a mile, I would . . .
- **a.** race to the finish line in hopes of being first.
- **b.** steadily make my way until I safely crossed the finish line.
- **c.** stay back to run along with a slower friend who needed support.
- **d.** laugh it off if I came in last place.

**5.** My biggest fear is . . .
- **a.** getting a bad grade.
- **b.** letting someone down.
- **c.** missing a game-winning shot.
- **d.** losing my friends.

**6.** The quote that describes me best is . . .
- **a.** "Go big or go home."
- **b.** "If I can dream it, I can do it."
- **c.** "There is no 'I' in 'TEAM.'"
- **d.** "The journey is half the fun."

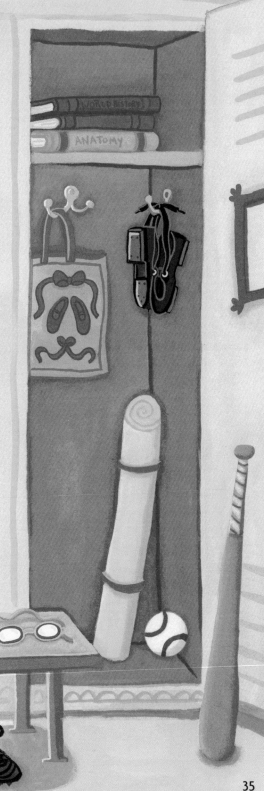

**7.** If a friend asked me to try out for the school play, I would . . .
  **a.** start memorizing the script that night.
  **b.** promise to try out as long as she'd give me some acting lessons.
  **c.** say, "No, thanks," and promise to watch her on opening night.
  **d.** give it a shot—it might be a lot of fun!

**8.** When my teacher passes back tests, I . . .
  **a.** ask around to see how everyone did compared to how I did.
  **b.** am happy with my grade because I studied hard.
  **c.** keep my grade to myself so that I don't hurt anyone's feelings.
  **d.** ask a friend if she'd like me to tutor her after I see her bad grade.

# Which Era Are You?

Do you sometimes think you should have grown up in another time? Find out which decade fits your dreams.

**1.** If something were to magically appear in my closet, I would want it to be a . . .
a. poodle skirt.
b. ball gown.
c. peace-sign necklace.
d. space suit.

**2.** Instead of sitting in class, sometimes I'd rather be . . .
a. watching movies.
b. making crafts.
c. listening to music.
d. playing on my computer.

**3.** If I could raise money for a charity, it would go to . . .
a. U.S. troops overseas.
b. the arts.
c. saving the planet.
d. scientific research.

**4.** In my free time, I'd prefer to . . .
a. host a formal tea party.
b. sew my own clothes.
c. work in a community garden.
d. make my own website.

**5.** I believe that I will someday . . .
a. star on Broadway.
b. run an art museum.
c. use solar energy at home.
d. travel to the moon.

**6.** When it comes to fashion, I'd most like to dress as . . .
a. an old-Hollywood movie star with pin curls and red lipstick.
b. a queen with layers of petticoats and interesting hats.
c. a prairie girl with a floral-print cotton dress.
d. a futuristic pop star with a light-up jacket.

**7.** I'd like to learn how to . . .
   **a.** swing dance.
   **b.** waltz.
   **c.** disco dance.
   **d.** moonwalk.

**8.** It would be interesting to live during a time when . . .
   **a.** there were no TVs or computers.
   **b.** people used horses instead of cars for transportation.
   **c.** we first landed on the moon.
   **d.** I could teleport anywhere in the world instantly.

**9.** One day, it would be awesome to meet . . .
   **a.** a movie star I admire.
   **b.** a rock star.
   **c.** the President.
   **d.** my favorite science-fiction author.

**10.** If there were a soundtrack to my life, it would be . . .
   **a.** all the top hits on the radio.
   **b.** personally written by me— I play an instrument.
   **c.** filled with meaningful lyrics and moving music.
   **d.** the music from a video game.

# Which Chef Are You?

Coming right up! Take this quiz to see which role you'd play best in the kitchen.

**1.** People tell me that I'm a . . .
   **a.** great listener.
   **b.** creative thinker.
   **c.** natural leader.
   **d.** reliable friend.

**2.** I could see myself one day . . .
   **a.** planning events.
   **b.** creating my own ice cream flavor.
   **c.** running a big company.
   **d.** being an assistant to someone famous.

**3.** One of the qualities I like about myself is that I'm . . .
   **a.** a friendly girl who gets along with everyone.
   **b.** a thoughtful person who pays attention to details.
   **c.** a well-rounded person who's interested in math and art.
   **d.** an organized girl who's always on time.

**4.** If I were to work in a restaurant, I think it would be most fun to . . .
   **a.** meet my customers and see how they like the food.
   **b.** create a space with a hip or funky vibe.
   **c.** design the menu and come up with new recipes.
   **d.** prepare all of the delicious food.

**5.** The part I like best about going out to eat is . . .
   **a.** helping my little brother order.
   **b.** choosing the dessert—so many yummy options!
   **c.** calculating the tip—I have a trick for figuring it out.
   **d.** thinking about how to re-create the recipes at home.

**6.** The food I serve at my upcoming birthday party will be . . .
   a. a menu my friends will love—I asked what they like.
   b. fresh-baked goods made with love.
   c. themed to match my decorations perfectly.
   d. made by my friends—I'm asking them to help me decorate the cupcakes!

**7.** At the charity bake sale, I'm the one most likely to . . .
   a. greet customers and ask them what flavors they like.
   b. bring a pretty tablecloth and extra sprinkles for the cupcakes.
   c. put up the posters AND handle the money.
   d. assign everyone at the table a task to make sure the sale runs smoothly.

**8.** There's nothing I love more than . . .
   a. putting a smile on someone's face.
   b. making things with my hands.
   c. taking charge of a project.
   d. giving great advice.

**9.** When it comes to making decisions, I like to . . .
   a. do what makes everyone happy.
   b. take a risk and try something different.
   c. do what I know is best.
   d. think about all of my options carefully before deciding.

**10.** The best kind of food is . . .
   a. my mom's—she knows just what I like.
   b. from a bake shop in town—its doughnuts are the best!
   c. from my favorite restaurant—I love the atmosphere as much as the food.
   d. food that I made myself—even if it takes a lot of hard work!

39

# Which Student Are You?

Take this "test" to find out which school style defines you.
P.S. There are no wrong answers!

**1.** A big project is due tomorrow, and I haven't started yet. I'd probably . . .
a. get really upset, because I usually don't forget things like this.
b. call my friends to make sure they didn't forget, either.
c. get started, because I can finish homework pretty quickly.
d. not worry—I already have a few ideas in my head.

**2.** In class, I'm great at . . .
a. setting a good example.
b. following directions perfectly.
c. answering questions about current events.
d. offering my artistic skills for projects.

**3.** When it comes to after-school activities, I've thought of . . .
a. running for student-council president.
b. tutoring younger students who need help.
c. entering the geography bee.
d. joining the poetry club.

**4.** My teachers know that I'll . . .
a. turn in my homework on time.
b. ask a question if I don't understand something.
c. participate in class.
d. write interesting, creative papers.

**5.** Once I had a dream that I was a . . .
 a. record-breaking swimmer.
 b. popular teacher.
 c. game-show contestant.
 d. children's book author.

**6.** If I get stuck on a math problem, I . . .
 a. practice a few similar ones so that I'll get the hang of it.
 b. ask the teacher for help so that she can talk me through it.
 c. pause for a moment so that I can remember how to do it.
 d. come up with an acronym to help me remember it next time.

**7.** When I study for a test, I prefer to . . .
 a. study by myself.
 b. study with friends so that I can talk through questions.
 c. make flash cards and ask a parent to quiz me.
 d. rewrite key facts from my notes.

**8.** Sometimes I wish I went to a school that had . . .
 a. no grades—I would still work just as hard.
 b. more group projects.
 c. verbal tests, such as what you'd see on a game show.
 d. music playing in the halls.

**9.** You won't find me at school without my . . .
 a. assignment notebook to help me stay organized.
 b. lucky pencil for taking great class notes.
 c. total concentration on the teacher's lessons.
 d. notebook for doodling while I listen in class.

**10.** The teacher often asks me to . . .
 a. help her pass out papers.
 b. answer another student's question.
 c. try out for the spelling bee.
 d. enter my projects in an art show.

# Which Country Are You?

Don't know where to go? See where your interests lead you.

**1.** In my room, you'll find . . .
  a. my collections on display.
  b. a basket of markers and colored pencils.
  c. bold colors on the walls and a ton of clothes.
  d. an MP3 player and enough space for a dance party.

**2.** If I could move anywhere in the world, I would move to a . . .
  a. small town with cute shops and restaurants.
  b. pretty countryside with great views.
  c. big city with lots of people.
  d. beach with beautiful blue ocean waters.

**3.** When I go on vacation, I like to . . .
  a. see historic sites I've read about at school.
  b. visit museums with hands-on exhibits.
  c. try new foods whose names I can't even pronounce.
  d. see a show or sporting event.

**4.** Everyone knows that I'm great at . . .
  a. playing any game—I'm a reliable teammate.
  b. art—I always think of unique ideas.
  c. putting together outfits— I like to be different.
  d. acting—I love to star in school plays.

**5.** The most fun part of my school day is . . .
  a. lunch, where I can catch up with my friends.
  b. art class, because I love to create.
  c. recess, during which I organize fun games.
  d. music class, because I get to perform.

**6.** At a party, I'm the girl who . . .
  a. introduces all the guests to one another.
  b. brings a treat that I made myself.
  c. is wearing the most original outfit.
  d. is entertaining everyone with my stories.

**7.** A new girl is standing by herself at recess. I . . .
  a. ask her a few questions about herself.
  b. tell her a fun fact about each of my friends.
  c. compliment her cool shoes.
  d. invite her to join in the game I'm playing.

**8.** My dream birthday party is one at which . . .
  a. my friends and I have a professional photo shoot.
  b. I design my own cake and a real chef bakes it.
  c. my friends and I go out for a fancy night in a sparkling downtown.
  d. I can do karaoke on a real stage.

**9.** Some days, I wish I could take a break from school and . . .
  a. just relax—I'm so busy.
  b. make craft projects all day.
  c. take a trip to the mall.
  d. try out for a reality TV show.

**10.** Even when I'm feeling down, I remind myself that . . .
  a. my friends and family love me more than anything.
  b. I need to get going again because nothing can stop me.
  c. no one's smile shines like mine.
  d. no one can rain on my parade.

# Which Pattern Are You?

Pick whether you like "this" or "that," and we'll tell you which pattern was woven just for you.

**1.** My go-to hairstyle is . . .
   **a.** a simple ponytail.
   **b.** a twist with a pretty barrette.
   **c.** my hair down with a plain headband.
   **d.** a messy fishtail braid.

**2.** If I had to dress up, I'd wear . . .
   **a.** pants and a button-up shirt.
   **b.** a skirt with tights and boots.
   **c.** my favorite dress and matching sweater.
   **d.** a shirt with a drawstring waist and colorful bracelets.

**3.** If you find a pile of notebooks, you'll know mine is the one with . . .
   **a.** my name printed simply on the front.
   **b.** sparkly stickers on the cover and my first name written in curly letters.
   **c.** a printed name label on the inside front cover.
   **d.** doodles all over it.

**4.** For school, you'll most likely find me wearing a . . .
   **a.** T-shirt and sneakers.
   **b.** jeweled tank top and a cardigan.
   **c.** polo shirt and capri pants.
   **d.** layered look, such as a skirt over leggings.

**5.** In my bedroom, I would love to add a . . .
   **a.** video-game console with special game-playing chairs.
   **b.** canopy bed with pretty curtains.
   **c.** white wooden desk with a matching chair.
   **d.** gigantic mural of an underwater scene.

**6.** When it comes to my feet, I prefer to step into . . .
   **a.** gym shoes.
   **b.** silver ballet flats.
   **c.** slip-on sneakers.
   **d.** beaded moccasins.

**8.** Guaranteed, you would never find me wearing . . .
   **a.** a frilly pink dress.
   **b.** dirty gym shoes.
   **c.** mismatched socks.
   **d.** a plain white T-shirt.

**9.** On my bed, you're likely to find . . .
   **a.** a matching blanket and pillow set.
   **b.** my teddy bear and a sequined pillow.
   **c.** pillows and sheets with my initials embroidered on them.
   **d.** a candy-shaped pillow and piles of stuffed animals.

**7.** To keep warm in the winter, I like to wear a . . .
   **a.** knit hat with a pompom on top.
   **b.** pair of fuzzy earmuffs.
   **c.** matching scarf and hat set.
   **d.** fun snowboarding cap with different-colored spikes.

**10.** If I had to describe my style in one word, it would be . . .
   **a.** comfortable.
   **b.** cute.
   **c.** classic.
   **d.** fun.

# Which Gadget Are You?

You may not be able to see into the future, but you can see which creative contraption your personality points to.

**1.** If I were to create an invention for the future, it would be . . .
- a. a system my friends could use to teleport into my room.
- b. digital wallpaper that changed with the touch of a button.
- c. a camera robot that followed me around and filmed my every move.
- d. a ceiling movie screen that could appear above my bed.

**2.** Even in the future, I think girls will still . . .
- a. play board games—classic games will never get old.
- b. read books—who doesn't love to get lost in a good story?
- c. listen to music—everyone loves to sing and dance.
- d. make crafts—creativity will never go out of style.

**3.** If I were a robot, I would be one that . . .
- a. greets students at the entrance of a school.
- b. grades papers and tests.
- c. works as a DJ at school dances and assemblies.
- d. paints huge murals inside and outside schools.

**4.** My favorite website is the kind that has . . .
- a. a place for me to create a profile and connect with friends.
- b. tons of music that I can listen to for free.
- c. multiplayer games.
- d. how-to videos that teach me new skills.

**5.** If I had my own online show, I would . . .

a. create a weekly report about what's new at school.

b. interview interesting friends and family members.

c. star in videos that got popular at school.

d. teach others how to do something.

**6.** In the future, I could see myself as the . . .

a. head news reporter on the moon.

b. teacher on a middle-school space station.

c. creator of the most popular video game ever.

d. owner of the first-ever art gallery in space.

**7.** I use the family computer mostly to . . .

a. e-mail my faraway friends and relatives.

b. do schoolwork.

c. play games.

d. upload pictures.

**8.** You'll never find me . . .

a. by myself. I love to surround myself with friends.

b. in the spotlight. I prefer to stay behind the scenes.

c. without an audience. I like to make people laugh.

d. bored. I can entertain myself for hours.

**9.** My favorite part of the weekend is when I'm . . .

a. hanging out with a few good friends.

b. curling up with a good story.

c. competing in a game or sport.

d. working on an art project.

**10.** I think one of my best qualities is that I . . .

a. can get along with anyone.

b. am a great listener.

c. am not afraid to act silly.

d. form my own opinions.

# Which Bag Are You?

You won't have to dig too deep to discover which carryall fits your character.

**1.** On my desk you'll find . . .
  a. an assignment notebook. I like to stay organized.
  b. a mess of schoolwork, dirty socks, and a tennis trophy.
  c. a matching pencil cup and paper tray.
  d. my sketchbook.

**2.** After school, I . . .
  a. finish my homework just in time for dinner.
  b. head straight for sports practice.
  c. hang out with a few friends before I study for my test.
  d. am up for anything fun—I need a little break after school.

**3.** In group work, I'm the girl who . . .
  a. takes charge.
  b. is the hardest worker.
  c. wants the final project to look perfect.
  d. loves hearing everyone's ideas.

**4.** On school picture day, I made sure that I wore my . . .
  a. glasses, because they make me look smart.
  b. school T-shirt, because I like to show my pride.
  c. top that matches my best friend's—we're like twins!
  d. beaded necklace that I made myself.

**5.** When we're playing team sports in gym class, I . . .
  a. make sure that everyone is following the rules.
  b. am the star player who's leading the team to victory.
  c. know everyone's first and last name on the team.
  d. am the one who came up with the team's goofy nickname.

**6.** If I had a locker, it would have . . .
  a. a calendar with important dates filled in.
  b. an extra pair of socks and a hair band.
  c. pictures of friends and my family.
  d. a pretty poster torn from my favorite magazine.

**7.** I once had a bad dream that I . . .
- a. flunked a test.
- b. broke my leg and missed the championship game.
- c. showed up at school wearing my little brother's dinosaur pajamas.
- d. lost the bracelet my best friend made for me.

**8.** My friends know they can ask me for . . .
- a. help on homework—I'm very studious.
- b. spare change or a spare pencil—I'm always prepared.
- c. advice—I like to help out my buddies.
- d. an idea—I'm full of them.

**9.** When it comes to losing things, I . . .
- a. never do, because all of my things have a special place.
- b. don't lose things—sometimes I just can't find them!
- c. keep a close eye on important things.
- d. am known to misplace things occasionally.

# Which Story Are You?

Everyone has a story to tell, but how would you tell yours? Take this quiz to reveal which story style is for you.

1. Friends say that you have a way with . . .
   a. others—you're usually surrounded by people.
   b. advice—they love hearing your thoughts.
   c. words—you can weave together interesting phrases.
   d. stories—you can make anything sound interesting.

2. When watching TV, you'd rather see . . .
   a. funny clips from one of those home-video shows.
   b. a talent competition— you like rooting for the underdog.
   c. music videos—you love song lyrics.
   d. your favorite series from start to finish on DVD.

3. When you read a new book, you tend to . . .
   a. discuss it with a few friends after you've finished.
   b. flip to the back of the book to read the ending first.
   c. read slowly, because you love to get lost in a book.
   d. read it from cover to cover in one sitting.

4. To you, the best part of a book is the . . .
   a. cast of characters— they're like friends.
   b. action—it's the reason a book is hard to put down!
   c. setting—you wish you could live in a fictional land.
   d. story—one day you'll write your own.

**5.** You just got back from vacation. You tell your friends about . . .
  **a.** the people you met and friends you made.
  **b.** your first snorkeling adventure.
  **c.** all the beautiful sites you visited.
  **d.** how your family almost missed your flight—with all the hilarious details.

**6.** Your friends are impressed by how . . .
  **a.** many other friends you have—everyone knows you!
  **b.** athletic you are.
  **c.** smart and creative you are.
  **d.** many interesting places you've visited.

**7.** If you could be famous one day, you'd want to be . . .
  **a.** an actress who stars in a great movie.
  **b.** a world-record breaker.
  **c.** a scientist who cured a disease.
  **d.** a talk-show host.

**8.** You're the kind of girl who likes to remember things by . . .
  **a.** posting pictures on a family blog or website.
  **b.** displaying memorabilia and souvenirs in your room.
  **c.** writing everything in a diary.
  **d.** talking to friends about your memories.

**9.** You couldn't survive one week without . . .
  **a.** seeing your friends—you'd miss them too much!
  **b.** seeing anyone—being all alone would be way too boring!
  **c.** reading—it's one of your favorite hobbies!
  **d.** talking—you almost always have something to say!

# Which Website Are You?

Everyone can be an expert on something. Find out which of your interests translates into a super site.

1. Your friends come to you when they're looking for advice about . . .
   a. how to survive the mile run in gym class.
   b. which song they should buy next.
   c. where to buy the best birthday gifts.
   d. how to beat the latest video game.

2. When you have some downtime, you like to . . .
   a. go for a bike ride with your family.
   b. watch TV.
   c. try out a new hairstyle.
   d. surf the web.

3. For the next school play, you'd sign up to . . .
   a. be a dancer and singer in the chorus.
   b. hang posters and run the ticket booth.
   c. design the set and organize the costumes.
   d. work the curtain and the lights.

4. The best birthday present you could get is tickets to see . . .
   a. your hometown sports team.
   b. a rock band in concert.
   c. a fashion show.
   d. any movie in 3-D.

**5.** One item in your room that you're pretty attached to is . . .
- a. a pair of good-luck socks you wear to every game.
- b. the giant movie poster from your favorite film.
- c. a framed photo you took yourself.
- d. an MP3 player that holds your song collection.

**6.** When it comes to reading, you prefer to . . .
- a. listen to an audiobook so that you can multitask.
- b. pick up a popular book series that everyone is reading.
- c. flip through magazines with lots of pretty pics.
- d. read on an e-reader or computer.

**7.** When you lose focus at school, it might be because you are daydreaming about . . .
- a. tonight's gymnastics practice and your back walkover.
- b. what it would be like to be friends with a glamorous celebrity.
- c. the new outfit that you're going to wear to school tomorrow.
- d. the new virtual-world website you found last night.

**8.** If you had the chance, you would definitely sign up to be . . .
- a. a mascot at your school's basketball games.
- b. an extra in a Hollywood movie being filmed in your town.
- c. a model at a local boutique.
- d. a video-game tester.

**9.** A typical birthday party of yours involves . . .
- a. an activity that gets you moving, such as ice-skating.
- b. a sleepover complete with popcorn and movies.
- c. a creative craft such as making beaded necklaces.
- d. a competitive game such as laser tag—and you'll win!

**10.** You get most excited or inspired when you hear a story about . . .
- a. an underdog who came out on top.
- b. a popular celebrity who started her own charity.
- c. a tip or trick that will make your life easier.
- d. a behind-the-scenes look at how something was made.

# Answers

# Which City Are You?

If you picked **mostly a's,** you're . . .
New York City.
Fast-paced and ambitious, you're a go-getter who likes to get things done. You're not afraid to try new things and take chances, and that's what New York City is all about. Big crowds? No worries. You'll find a way to stand out!

If you picked **mostly b's,** you're . . .
Los Angeles.
You're a girl who follows her dreams. Your laid-back attitude and positive outlook give you a California vibe that fits in perfectly in Los Angeles. When you're not following your dreams, you love to follow the sound of waves crashing on the beach. Relaxing comes naturally to you, and your friends feel calm around you.

If you picked **mostly c's,** you're . . .
Denver.
As an active girl, you can't hold back your love for fresh air and the great outdoors. You like working hard and reaping the rewards, like hiking to the top of a mountain and then enjoying the beautiful view. You can find fun in any situation—or any weather—and that's what your friends love most about you.

If you picked **mostly d's,** you're . . .
Atlanta.
The South is known for its friendliness and charm—just like you! You feel comfortable talking to anyone, which means you easily make friends wherever you go. It's no surprise that you love to surround yourself with the people you care about most. Family and friends are drawn to you!

# Which Cupcake Are You?

If you picked **mostly a's,** you're a . . .
Rainbow-Sprinkled Cupcake.
You're the life of the party, just like a cupcake with a burst of rainbow sprinkles. You've found that there's nothing a smile or a laugh can't improve. You're not afraid to be the center of attention or to make a statement. If anything goes wrong, you can laugh it off and look on the bright side.

If you picked **mostly b's,** you're a . . .
Cupcake with Raspberry Filling.
You may be shy on the outside, but inside there's a surprise—you're a super-creative person. You just like to express yourself in quiet ways, and it takes you a little while to warm up to others. Friends know that when you do speak up, you always have something interesting to say.

If you picked **mostly c's,** you're a . . .
Pupcake.
You can't help it—you love animals! Your kindness toward others—and their pets—shows through in all aspects of your life. A sweet friend who loves to care for others, you'll never leave someone behind. You're not happy unless everyone around you is happy, too.

If you picked **mostly d's,** you're a . . .
Vanilla Cupcake.
Vanilla might seem plain, but actually it's a reliable, goes-with-everything flavor—and you're a true friend! Your buddies know that they can count on you in times of need. That's why you have so many special people in your life. Remember, they'll be there to return the favor when you need it.

# Which Movie Style Are You?

If you picked **mostly a's,** you're an . . .
Adventure Film.
You might be sitting still in the theater seat, but your mind is racing! You love action, adventure, and heroes who save the day. That's probably why you're a natural leader who's ready to help a friend in need.

If you picked **mostly b's,** you're a . . .
Romance Flick.
Happy endings are what you love most. You're an optimist and a dreamer—two qualities your friends and family love about you. You like to surround yourself with good people, good fun, and good stories.

If you picked **mostly c's,** you're a . . .
Scary Movie.
Not only are you not afraid of anything, but you're a prankster as well. You make your friends jump, but it's all in good fun. In fact, you're really great at laughing off anything. Others love your spirited outlook.

If you picked **mostly d's,** you're a . . .
Mystery Motion Picture.
If you're given a problem, you'll solve it! You're a trivia master who has the focus to tackle a tricky puzzle. Your friends know your smarts will take you far, and that's why they turn to you for advice.

# Which Art Supply Are You?

If you picked **mostly a's,** you're . . . Oil Paints.
Trying something new makes you a little nervous, so oil paints are just the supply you need. By mixing colors and brushes, you can mess around without messing up. When it comes to being creative, there's never a wrong approach—so trust your gut and don't be afraid to make your own decisions.

If you picked **mostly b's,** you're . . . Clay.
What's great about you is that you can mold something from nothing—just as with clay! Certain creative challenges can be a little scary, but you know that you can work through them and come up with something great. And you always have fun doing it.

If you picked **mostly c's,** you're . . . Markers.
When it comes to making art, you like to keep it simple and classic. You prefer to be creative in a way that you feel familiar with. You take inspiration from the world and then add your own spin. Don't be afraid to let your own creativity shine.

If you picked **mostly d's,** you're . . . Glitter.
Some have a green thumb, but you have a glitter thumb! There's no creative challenge that you can't overcome. You like to be loud and a little over-the-top. With your sparkling creativity, there's no telling what you'll come up with next. Everyone loves your unique ideas.

# Which Video Game Are You?

If you picked **mostly a's,** you're a . . . Karaoke Game.

For you, performing is easy! You're confident and talented, which is why you love a video game that lets you put on a show for your friends. You like to be the center of attention or the star player—your team can rely on you to take the winning shot.

If you picked **mostly b's,** you're a . . . Dance Game.

You like to have fun—and get a little silly—when you play games. Dance video games let you try something new with a group of friends, and what can be more entertaining? You're not worried about winning. You know that if you practice hard enough, you can always improve. And that's a winning attitude.

If you picked **mostly c's,** you're a . . . Race-Car Game.

Competitive? Daring? That's you! You love to chase a big win—it's the reason that race-car video games are perfect for you. You thrive under pressure, especially when you're facing other talented people. They inspire you to push yourself to a new level—and to win another game!

If you picked **mostly d's,** you're a . . . Trivia Game.

You're a patient problem solver whose brain is full of information—which means you're also a trivia queen. You love games that make you think. Besides your endless knowledge of random facts, your creative-thinking skills help you tackle every puzzle you encounter.

# Which Drink Are You?

If you picked **mostly a's,** you're a . . .
Peanut Butter & Banana Milk Shake.
A shake mixed with a scoop of peanut butter and a banana is exactly the kind of sweet that satisfies your desire for savory flavor. Although you might prefer a sandwich with potato chips crushed inside, try adding a fruit or vegetable to your favorite meals. Lettuce in sandwiches, broccoli in mac and cheese, and peppers on pizza are healthy additions that taste yummy.

If you picked **mostly b's,** you're a . . .
Strawberry Parfait.
For you, it's all about sweets! You haven't met one that you didn't like. Chocolate, candy, and cupcakes taste great, but remember to balance all that sugar with something healthy. Replace soda and candy with fruit and fruit juice—they're just as sweet and delicious!

If you picked **mostly c's,** you're . . .
Chocolate Milk.
Some might call you a picky eater, but you'd say that you know what you like. Don't limit yourself to only your favorite foods, though—there are sure to be new things out there that you'll love. Try filling your plate with at least three different colors at every meal. Think green for lettuce, brown for chicken, and red for tomatoes.

If you picked **mostly d's,** you're a . . .
Triple-Berry Smoothie.
To you, eating is an adventure! You're not afraid of any food, even something that looks a little weird—you might love it! You do a great job of eating balanced meals and healthy snacks. But it's OK to eat a treat every once in a while, too.

# Which Plant Are You?

If you picked **mostly a's,** you're . . .
Bamboo.
Strong and independent, you're never afraid to speak
your mind or stand up for yourself—or for others who
need your help. Because you're so independent, you
have some different interests from your friends, and that
makes you special. You know that following your heart is
right for you.

If you picked **mostly b's,** you're an . . .
Orchid.
You like simple but beautiful things, like elegant
orchids. Some people may tell you that you're wise
beyond your years—maybe it's because you don't
mind being alone and have always seemed mature.
Your friends respect your judgment and the way you
can keep calm under pressure. They turn to you in
tough situations.

If you picked **mostly c's,** you're a . . .
Sunflower.
Nothing is brighter than a sunflower on a beautiful day.
You love to be active outside—it always puts you in
a good mood, and it turns out that good moods are
contagious! Your friends love being around your positive
attitude and big smile. You inspire them to be a little
more carefree.

If you picked **mostly d's,** you're . . .
Ivy.
Just like ivy, your interests spread far and wide. Your
friends would call you an all-around superstar for your
involvement in school, sports, and clubs. You just love
to be a part of something and can never turn down an
opportunity. When it comes to trying something new,
you're fearless!

# Which Animal Are You?

If you picked **mostly a's,** you're a . . .
Golden Retriever.
Your ears perk up when your family is around, just like a friendly family pup! Your playfulness is contagious, but sometimes you like to take it easy and just hang out. You understand other people's feelings and have a way of making them feel calm and happy. It's a great quality to have!

If you picked **mostly b's,** you're a . . .
Palomino Horse.
Your friends don't know anyone as dedicated and hardworking as you are. You live a fast-paced life, filled with energy, activities, and lots of time on the court or field. Your determination means that you're also a little competitive—nothing fires you up more than the thought of winning!

If you picked **mostly c's,** you're a . . .
Calico Cat.
Just like a cat, you're an independent creature. You never have a problem taking care of yourself or entertaining yourself—in fact, that's how you prefer it! You get along well with everyone, but you prefer to relax with a good book or calming music. It's easy for you to drift away into your own world.

If you picked **mostly d's,** you're a . . .
Tropical Fish.
Fish travel in *schools* (or groups), and so do you! You're usually surrounded by a posse of close friends, and when you're not, it's easy for you to make new ones. When it comes to swimming, you're practically a fish! You're a natural in any body of water.

# Which Experiment Are You?

If you picked **mostly a's,** you're an . . .
Erupting-Volcano Experiment.
When it comes to experiments, you're kind of a mad
scientist—you like to mix things, take chances, and see
what happens! Most important, you like to put your
own personal stamp on everything you do. Your
creativity makes you memorable—you always
stand out in a crowd.

If you picked **mostly b's,** you're a . . .
Crystal-Growing Experiment.
A project like this takes dedication, patience, and
time. You're willing to work long hours for a great
payoff in the end, whether it's in school, sports, or
science. Friends are amazed by your ability to stay
focused and wowed by the cool things you create.

If you picked **mostly c's,** you're a . . .
Penny-in-Soda Experiment.
An experiment like this always surprises onlookers—
as well as you! You like learning interesting and useful
information, and then sharing it with people. After
all, experiments like this can make a difference—your
classmates may drink a lot less soda after seeing what it
can do to a penny.

If you picked **mostly d's,** you're a . . .
Slime Experiment.
You see a science fair as a chance to have fun! You're
not afraid to get a little dirty—and silly—especially
when you're learning something new. You'd prefer
to spend your time making something that you can
use or play with later. It's like a souvenir of your
hard work!

# Which Accessory Are You?

If you picked **mostly a's,** you're a . . .
Locket Necklace.
It's fine to be shy. Just like a locket, you keep things to yourself. You might try something new in private—such as a cool hairstyle or fun dance—but you don't take too many chances in public. Find a group of friends that will support you no matter what. Then you can let your true self shine with confidence!

If you picked **mostly b's,** you're . . .
Fingerless Gloves.
You know who you are! Your friends admire the fact that you're not afraid to try something new—even if you mess up or look silly doing it. Your boldness gives you strength to be yourself no matter what others think. Keep being YOU, and you'll go far.

If you picked **mostly c's,** you're . . .
Post Earrings.
As an easygoing girl, you like routine and keep things simple. You play it a little safe, but it's mostly because you don't overthink things. If something is working for you, why change it? Don't hide your personality, though—it's OK to shine in new ways sometimes.

If you picked **mostly d's,** you're a . . .
Purple Scarf.
Not only are you a trendsetter, but you're also a role model to your friends and siblings. They look up to you because you're smart, friendly, and confident. A little compliment from you goes a long way. Be sure to encourage your friends to let their personalities shine, too.

# Which Word Are You?

If you picked mostly a's, you're . . .
Sprightly. (Say it: SPRYT-lee. It means "spirited.")
Your bubbling energy is contagious! When your friends are around, they have a good time thanks to your bright smiles and positive outlook. You like to make others happy even if doing that makes you look a little goofy—it's worth it!

If you picked mostly b's, you're . . .
Loquacious. (Say it: low-QWAY-shuss. It means "talkative.")
Yep, you like to talk. You love conversation and sharing information with others. That means you don't mind speaking in public, either, whether you're performing onstage or giving a speech. This skill will take you far. Just remember that sometimes it's better to keep quiet—such as when someone is telling you something important!

If you picked mostly c's, you're . . .
Nimble. (Say it: NIHM-bull. It means "agile.")
Athletic and smart, you're a quick thinker who moves with ease. You show your cleverness in all your activities, whether it's while reading a textbook or playing a soccer game. You work hard and love to win, and you encourage your friends to do the same. But don't forget—the journey is half the fun!

If you picked mostly d's, you're . . .
Convivial. (Say it: kun-VIV-ee-ull. It means "agreeable.")
When it comes to being friendly, you're about as sweet as they come. You put others before yourself and are aware of how your actions affect your friends' feelings. You'd never want to let a friend down. Because of this, new friends flock to you all the time—what's not to like?

# Which Volunteer Are You?

If you picked **mostly a's,** you're an . . .
Animal-Shelter Volunteer.
You love to help others—especially the furry critters.
See what kind of food and supplies your local animal
shelter needs as donations, or ask your family if all of
you can sign up to help walk pets on the weekends.
Organizing a craft sale or bake sale could raise money for
the local animal shelter, too!

If you picked **mostly b's,** you're a . . .
Marathon Volunteer.
You're super friendly and supportive. Passing out
water on the sidelines of a race and cheering on
the competitors is fun, and it makes you feel good,
too. Marathon runners work hard and appreciate
encouragement from helpers like you. Maybe you'll get
inspired to run a long-distance race yourself one day.

If you picked **mostly c's,** you're a . . .
Food-Pantry Volunteer.
Food pantries always need help and supplies. Check
online to see exactly what the pantry is looking for,
or ask a parent if you can go in to help organize the
incoming donations, discard expired food, or deliver
supplies in your community. Every little bit can make
a big difference for a lot of people!

If you picked **mostly d's,** you're a . . .
Nature Volunteer.
You *can* help make the world a better place! Science
museums, local nature preserves, and public parks all
need volunteers. There are lots of ways to get your
whole family involved, from helping keep green spaces
clean to planting new flowers to grooming hiking
trails. And you can help the environment by recycling,
conserving electricity, and reusing items when possible.

# Which Vacation Are You?

If you picked **mostly a's**, you're a . . .
South American Cruise.
You'll try anything new as long as your family is by your side. With just a little coaxing and encouragement, you'll overcome any fears. The comfort of a cruise ship lets you explore amazing new places but return to the same bed every night. You know that you can have fun anywhere—it's the people you are with who make the trip great.

If you picked **mostly b's**, you're a . . .
European Backpacking Trip.
Adventure is your middle name! An unfamiliar city, a rainy day, or an unknown language doesn't stop you from discovering new places. You love to explore and, like a sponge, soak up information wherever you go. That makes you a street-smart traveler who's also a great leader.

If you picked **mostly c's**, you're a . . .
Caribbean Island Vacation.
When traveling, you love to take it easy and enjoy the sights and sounds around you. To you, the best vacations are for relaxing. You enjoy warm weather and soaking up the sun. This kind of trip is a nice escape from your usual busy schedule, and you come home feeling refreshed and happy.

If you picked **mostly d's**, you're a . . .
Camping Trek in Colorado.
There's no relaxing on this vacation—you're all about getting active and roughing it in the great outdoors. You want to put your skills to the test when you travel. Going for an extra-long hike, sleeping under the stars, and exploring a new place are the kinds of things that excite you.

# Which Character Are You?

If you picked **mostly a's,** you're a . . .
Wizard.
Maybe you don't know any magic spells or have a wand, but it sure seems as if you do! You're always coming up with great solutions to small and big problems for your friends and family. Save those ideas—one of them just might change the world!

If you picked **mostly b's,** you're a . . .
Superhero.
You're smart. You're strong. And you're loyal. Just like a comic-book hero! You don't need a cape or the ability to fly to save the day. Friends are impressed that you aren't afraid to speak your mind and stand up for others. If a friend is feeling down, you're by her side in an instant.

If you picked **mostly c's,** you're a . . .
Fairy.
You love to care, share, and be fair! You're a great girl who looks out for her friends—whether they know it or not. (Like a fairy godmother!) You love to see your friends succeed, so you go out of your way to cheer them on and cheer them up—whatever they need!

If you picked **mostly d's,** you're an . . .
Elf.
Your friends agree that you're wise beyond your years—and that's why they seek your advice. You are patient and kind, approachable and fun. You're a dreamer, but you also stay grounded in reality. That's where your creativity comes in—artistic projects are an escape and a way for you to express yourself.

# Which Ball Are You?

If you picked **mostly a's,** you're a . . . Volleyball.
No amount of tough competition can stop you. When you play a game, you have one goal: to win! Your talent and focused dedication shine through, which makes you a star. But don't get too down on yourself if you don't come out on top every time—there's more to life than winning.

If you picked **mostly b's,** you're a . . . Tennis Ball.
Just as a tennis ball gets volleyed back and forth and back and forth again, you never tire out. You work equally hard toward your dreams or for something you've never tried before. You've seen how dedication can pay off, and it's made you confident that you can tackle anything.

If you picked **mostly c's,** you're a . . . Soccer Ball.
Soccer is a team sport, and you're a great team player. You support your friends and your family without question, and you're considerate of others' feelings. Because you're involved with lots of activities, some might call you a social butterfly. Yep, it means you're busy, but it also makes you a well-rounded girl.

If you picked **mostly d's,** you're a . . . Playground Ball.
Games mean one thing to you—fun! With a group of good friends at your side, you're up for anything. After all, friendship is more important to you than winning. You'd much rather cheer on your friends than compete with them. Supporting others makes you happy, and that's a kind of winning in itself.

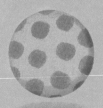

# Which Era Are You?

If you picked **mostly a's,** you're the . . .
1940s.
You love anything retro and glamorous—the 1940s are a perfect fit. Hollywood movie stars and classic all-American fashion are just a few things you love most about this decade. After all, some things—such as listening to the radio, seeing the latest movie, and being patriotic—are still as popular as ever!

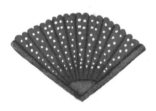

If you picked **mostly b's,** you're the . . .
1800s.
It was a time before computers and cars, movies, and cell phones, but with your patience and artistic abilities, you'd fit right in during the 1800s. You love the idea of "being a lady"—dressing up and attending a ball would be a dream come true. Maybe someday you'll get to do it in this decade!

If you picked **mostly c's,** you're the . . .
1970s.
When it comes to causes that affect the environment and your world, you like to get involved and make a difference. The 1970s would have been a perfect time for you to have lived. When you care about an issue, you take action—and persuade your friends to help, too.

If you picked **mostly d's,** you're the . . .
2030s.
The future is calling your name! You can't wait to see what it holds—will there be teleportation, vacations on the moon, or flying cars? You'll be ready for it all because you're not afraid to try new things and are an imaginative thinker. Who knows how you'll make your mark? You'll find out someday.

# Which Chef Are You?

If you picked **mostly a's,** you're a . . . Personal Chef.

You love meeting new people and learning all you can about them. You're a great listener and a thoughtful friend. Because of this, you'd be a wonderful personal chef. You'd create special menus and events, cook yummy food, and leave your clients satisfied. Their smiling faces would make you so happy!

If you picked **mostly b's,** you're a . . . Pastry Chef.

It's true that you love sweet treats. But more important, you're a super-creative girl who pushes the limits. You like to make things pretty with interesting details and have an artistic talent that your friends admire. Your desserts would taste great—and look great, too!

If you picked **mostly c's,** you're an . . . Executive Chef.

You're a natural leader, so Executive Chef is a great fit for you. You're a multitalented girl who likes art and math—a powerful mix. As Executive Chef, you'd have plenty of ideas for menus and restaurant designs. You'd also run the business, including hiring employees and managing money.

If you picked **mostly d's,** you're a . . . Sous-Chef. (Say it: SOO-shef. It means "assistant to the chef.")

You work hard, and organization and dedication are your star qualities. As Sous-Chef, you'd oversee the kitchen commotion by making schedules and answering questions. You're great at taking and giving directions, so friends respect you and listen to your advice.

# Which Student Are You?

If you picked **mostly a's,** you're a . . . Shining Star.

School is important to you, and your teacher can tell. You study hard and it pays off. Because of your great listening skills, complete homework assignments, and overall good grades, you set a great example for every student to follow. Let yourself have fun after school— joining a club or sport might balance your school efforts.

If you picked **mostly b's,** you're a . . . Handy Helper.

Your classmates can count on you to assist them in a pinch. You listen hard in class and ask smart questions, so you really grasp the lessons quickly—which means you can usually help others who are struggling. Your teacher notices the extra time you take to encourage your classmates. You're a great team player.

If you picked **mostly c's,** you're a . . . Quiz Master.

You're a fact whiz! Because of your great memory—and your competitive nature—you're usually the first to raise your hand. Your brain soaks up facts like a sponge, which makes homework and tests easier for you. If you haven't already, you should put your knowledge to the test in a geography or spelling bee—you'd be great!

If you picked **mostly d's,** you're a . . . Creative Queen.

You shine the most when using your imagination, such as by writing or drawing. Your teacher is impressed by your ideas and your willingness to share your creative talents with the class. If you haven't already, think of entering a story or artwork in a student contest— your teacher can help you find one. You might win an award!

# Which Country Are You?

If you picked **mostly a's,** you're . . . Canada.

You're an all-around great girl: friendly, fun, and smart. You know how to balance friendships and schoolwork but still make time for yourself. Friends trust you for your good judgment and wise words. You're a great role model for others.

If you picked **mostly b's,** you're . . . France.

You're a creativity connoisseur. From crafting art projects to creating concoctions in the kitchen, you're always filled with ideas. Friends know you'll always contribute something great, whether to school reports or bedroom decor.

If you picked **mostly c's,** you're . . . Japan.

You're innovative and original, and so is your style. Your just-right choices always show off the real you. Friends look up to you for your confidence and great ideas. It's inspiring!

If you picked **mostly d's,** you're . . . Brazil.

You love to be in the spotlight! You're always performing—whether you're just telling a joke at recess or winning a trophy with your soccer team. And for you, it's all fun. Friends know they'll have a great time when you're around.

# Which Pattern Are You?

If you picked **mostly a's,** you're . . .
Stripes.
Comfort is important to you, and stripes are simple, look cool, and never go out of style. You know what you like when it comes to fashion, and you stick to your favorites rather than experiment with trends. After all, they're your favorites for a reason!

If you picked **mostly b's,** you're . . .
Polka Dots.
"Cute" perfectly describes your style. You enjoy having some fun with accents such as sequins, jewels, and fur. More important, you like your personality and want to show it off. You wear only what says "YOU" to you!

If you picked **mostly c's,** you're . . .
Plaid.
Your style is smart and classic—a perfect match for plaid. Traditional and timeless is a reliable combination. You like things to be just so, and this preppy pattern goes perfectly with your particular personality.

If you picked **mostly d's,** you're . . .
Tie-Dye.
For you, fashion is fun and creative. You have many interests, and your style is a little unpredictable, just like a tie-dyed T-shirt. There's no right or wrong way to style yourself. Your motto is "Experiment!"

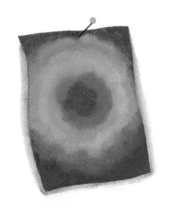

# Which Gadget Are You?

If you picked **mostly a's,** you're a . . .
Smartphone.
You stay connected with your friends. Whether you're sitting next to them at lunch or e-mailing them after school, you always know what's going on in their lives. You like to talk but also like to listen, which makes you a great friend. Just make sure you're talking to your friends in real life as much you're "talking" to them virtually!

If you picked **mostly b's,** you're a . . .
Music Player.
You're a little quiet on the outside, but your mind is a storehouse of interesting knowledge. And your good grades show it. Although you like to spend time alone reading or listening to music, your friends love to see you. Don't turn down an invite or be afraid to share your thoughts. You're a smart girl!

If you picked **mostly c's,** you're a . . .
Video-Game System.
Because you're so fun to be around, friends flock to you. There's no audience that you can't charm. Although you like to be the center of attention, be sure to let your friends shine, too. Use your natural talents to help them feel comfortable and give them a chance to speak up.

If you picked **mostly d's,** you're a . . .
Video Camera.
You're an original! Your creativity can be seen in all parts of your life—at school, in sports, and at home. Since you're easily inspired, why not encourage your friends to try their hands at something creative? Your can-do attitude is contagious.

# Which Bag Are You?

If you picked mostly a's, you're a . . .
Messenger Bag.
As a stellar student who loves to study, you have to stay organized—and that's the way you like it, anyway! At school and in life, you've found a perfect place for everything. And just as multiple compartments divide a messenger bag, you know how to divide your time between work and fun—a skill that amazes your friends.

If you picked mostly b's, you're a . . .
Backpack.
You're a busy girl who's always on the run. Whether you're going to school, band practice, swim team, or a friend's house, you like to keep everything close by—just in case! You might be a little disorganized sometimes, but don't sweat it. Your friends know how hard you work, and they're impressed by your involvement!

If you picked mostly c's, you're a . . .
Purse.
A social girl like you has to be able to pick up and go as she pleases. And you don't need to have a plan to feel comfortable, as long as you have a few friends (and some necessities) nearby. Just like a handbag, you're full of surprises. It's a quality your friends love about you.

If you picked mostly d's, you're a . . .
Tote Bag.
Creativity is your middle name! Your mind is filled with great ideas on the inside, and you like to show your uniqueness on the outside, too. A tote bag is like a blank canvas—it can hold anything and be decorated easily—which is exactly your style. Your friends are impressed by your original ideas.

# Which Story Are You?

If you picked **mostly a's,** you're a . . .
Magazine Feature.
Like a celebrity, you have tons of friends who want to know what's going on in your life. You're just so fun to be around! You know what's new with your friends and in pop culture. What can you say? You love people!

If you picked **mostly b's,** you're a . . .
Front-Page Newspaper Story.
"Breaking news" among your friends is usually starring you! Your friends look up to you because you're very talented in all that you do. They come to you for advice and listen carefully, because they know you have their best interests at heart.

If you picked **mostly c's,** you're a . . .
Poem.
You may be a little quiet, but you're smart and strong! You express yourself best not by talking but by being creative. That's why you can so easily get lost reading a book or drawing a picture. Your imagination is vibrant and makes you unique—never lose that quality.

If you picked **mostly d's,** you're a . . .
Novel.
You always have something to add to a conversation. You are especially great at entertaining friends with your interesting stories—sharing everything from funny moments to helpful advice. And you enjoy hearing stories, too. You're a great listener.

# Which Website Are You?

If you picked **mostly a's,** you're a . . .
Sports-News Website.
You like being active and winning games, and you love athletes' amazing stories of hard work and dedication. Your friends are inspired by your athletic abilities and courage. In fact, the first story on your website might feature YOU!

If you picked **mostly b's,** you're a . . .
Movie-Reviews Website.
Friends can always ask you for updates on the latest in TV, movie, and pop-culture news. You even know a lot about how movies are made and directed. Since you're so film-smart, you should try your hand at making your own movie!

If you picked **mostly c's,** you're a . . .
Fashion Blog.
You're a creative chica who loves beautiful things. Your friends admire your one-of-a-kind outfits, handmade accessories, and helpful tips on how to French-braid hair. A blog is the perfect place to share your quirky and stylish ideas with the world.

If you picked **mostly d's**, you're a . . .
Gadget Blog.
You love being the first to test the latest and greatest tech toys, from music players to cell phones to video games. You're a natural at using technology—your friends and family often ask you for help with their digital dilemmas. As the resident technology expert, your gadget guide could help many people!

# Which was your favorite quiz? Tell us!

Mail to:

*Which _____ Are You?* Editor
American Girl
8400 Fairway Place
Middleton, WI  53562

# Here are some other American Girl books you might like.

Each sold separately. Find more books online at americangirl.com.